You could glue one big collage heart onto a card, like the one above.

Try making a card with a collage background, like this green one.

6. Spread glue on the back of the hearts. Press one heart onto each rectangle on the card, then leave the glue to dry.

Tissue paper lovebirds

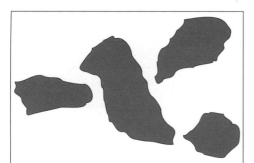

Brush the glue to the edges of the shapes.

1. Rip a shape for a lovebird's body from pink tissue paper. Then, rip two shapes for the wings and one for the tail, too.

2. Gently brush white glue on the back of the body. Press it onto a piece of white paper, then glue on the wings and tail.

You could draw a tree with heart-shaped leaves, for your lovebirds to perch on.

3. Rip another shape for a body and two shapes for wings from blue tissue paper. Then, glue them onto the paper, too.

4. Rip lots of small pieces from pink tissue paper. Glue them in the spaces around the lovebirds, then leave the glue to dry.

This will be the beak.

5. Using a black felt-tip pen, draw the lovebirds' bodies. You don't need to follow the edges of the tissue paper too closely.

Valentine Things to make and do

Rebecca Gilpin

Designed and illustrated by
Josephine Thompson, Katrina Fearn
and Vici Leyhane

Edited by Fiona Watt

Steps illustrated by Stella Baggott
Photographs by Howard Allman

Contents

SCHOLASTIC INC.
New York Toronto London Auckland Sydney
Mexico City New Delhi Hong Kong Buenos Aires

Bright hearts card

1. For a card, fold a piece of thick paper in half. Then, cut three rectangles from wrapping paper and glue them onto the card.

Find as many patterns as you can.

2. Rip lots of red and pink pieces from pictures in an old magazine. You could rip pieces from pink and red wrapping paper, too.

Use some of the ideas on these pages when you make your card.

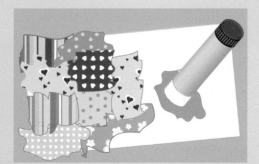

3. For the collage, glue the ripped pieces of paper all over a piece of thick white paper. Overlap the edges of the pieces.

4. Turn the collage over and draw three hearts on the back of it. Then, cut out the hearts, just inside the lines.

5. Glue each collage heart onto a piece of bright paper. Draw a bigger heart around each one, then cut along the lines.

Make a Valentine picture with lots of lovebirds flying around.

To make two lovebirds hug, glue the wing of one over the body of the other.

6. Draw a tail at the end of each lovebird's body. Then, draw the wings, legs and beaks. Add eyes and feathers on their heads.

7. Draw hearts on the small pieces of pink tissue paper. Then, draw tiny hearts on the lovebirds' bodies, too.

Pretty roses loveheart

Keep the paper folded as you cut.

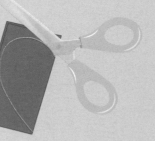

1. Fold a small piece of pink paper in half. Then, draw half a heart against the fold. Cut out the shape, then open out the heart.

2. Cut a rectangle that is about the size of a postcard from thick pink paper. Then, lay a pencil along one of the long edges.

For a Valentine decoration, glue several lovehearts onto a long ribbon.

3. Curl the paper tightly around the pencil. Then, roll the pencil up the paper to the top edge. Unroll it and remove the pencil.

Roll the paper on a flat surface.

4. Fold in the edge that was curled around the pencil, to make it easier to roll. Then, roll the paper again, as tightly as you can.

The slices get flattened by the scissors.

5. Cut the rolled paper into slices. Then, to make the slices look more like round roses, gently squash them a little.

Glue the rose near the edge of the heart.

6. Pour some white glue onto an old plate. Dip the bottom of a rose into it and press the rose onto the heart.

The lovehearts look pretty when glued onto a card, too.

You could glue a loveheart onto a little gift box.

If you need a few more roses, make another roll of paper.

7. Glue another rose next to the first one. Glue more roses around the edge of the heart, then glue the rest in the middle.

8. To make leaves, tightly fold a small piece of green paper, along its long edge, several times. Then, cut the folded paper into slices.

9. Dip a leaf into the glue and press it into a gap between two roses. Glue on lots more leaves, then leave the glue to dry.

Sparkly hearts garland

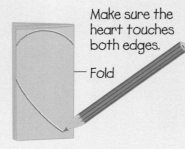

Make sure the heart touches both edges.

Fold

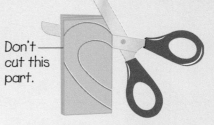

Don't cut this part.

1. Cut a long, thin strip of green paper. Then, fold it in half, with the short ends together. Crease the fold really well.

2. Fold the paper in half two more times. Then, draw half a heart on the folded paper, against the fold, like this.

3. Draw a second line inside the first one. Then, holding the layers together, carefully cut along the lines you have drawn.

To make a long garland, tape two or more garlands together.

To make hearts like these, draw a pointed shape in step 2, with a much smaller shape inside.

Flatten the garland.

4. Open out the garland and lay it on a newspaper. Then, mix some paint and white glue together on an old plate.

5. Paint stripes on one of the hearts. Sprinkle glitter over the wet paint. Then, paint around another heart and sprinkle it with glitter.

6. Shake any excess glitter onto the newspaper. Glue sequins or paper shapes onto the other hearts, then leave the garland to dry.

You could glue tiny beads onto some of the hearts, too.

Try painting different patterns, such as stars or circles, on the hearts.

Zigzag card

1. To make the card, fold a long rectangle of thick paper, like this. The front part should be narrower than the back part.

Fold

New fold

Back edge

2. Turn the paper over. Then, fold back the right-hand section, so that the new fold lines up with the back edge of the card.

You could decorate a tall card with a big heart and sequins.

Try adding extra sparkle with glitter glue.

Glue hearts along more than one edge of a card.

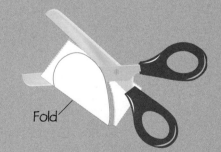

Cut off this part.

Fold

3. The front section should be about half of the width of the card. If it's wider, draw a pencil line down the card and cut along it.

4. To make the heart decorations, fold a piece of thick paper in half. Draw half a heart against the fold, then cut it out.

5. Open out the heart. Lay it on a piece of pink paper and draw around it. Then, draw around it twice more on other pieces of paper.

You could decorate a card with a flower made from hearts.

The little heart in the middle was brushed with glue and sprinkled with glitter.

This card had different shades of paper glued inside and on the front.

6. Cut out the hearts. Then, cut out another smaller heart from thick paper. Draw around it three times and cut out the shapes.

Only glue the left side of each heart.

7. Glue one small heart onto each big heart. Then, glue the big hearts along the edge on the front of the card, like this.

8. Brush lots of dots of white glue around the edges of the hearts and press on sequins. Then, leave the glue to dry.

Striped Valentine card

Leave white gaps between the stripes.

1. Pour some paint onto an old plate and mix it with a little water. Then, paint a thick line across a piece of white paper.

2. Using another shade of paint, add a second thick line. Then, paint lots of thin lines across the paper and leave the paint to dry.

3. With a red felt-tip pen, draw lots of small hearts on one of the lines. Outline the hearts with a black pen. Add some thin lines, too.

4. Using a gold pen, draw lots of tiny hearts and dots on some of the painted lines. Then, draw some gold lines, too.

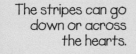

The stripes can go down or across the hearts.

5. Using a pencil, draw a big heart in the middle of the painting. Then, draw two smaller hearts, on other parts of the painting.

6. Cut out the hearts, just inside the lines. Make a card by folding a piece of thick paper in half, then glue the hearts on the front.

You could make
flowers with
single leaves, too.

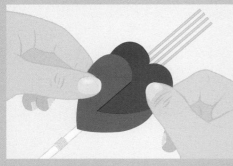

6. Hold the heart with the slot at the bottom, above the other heart. Then, push the slots in the hearts together, like this.

7. Fold a piece of thick paper in half and draw a leaf against the fold. Then, cut out the shape and glue the leaf onto the straw.

8. To finish off the flower, bend the thin green strips with your fingers. Then, thread small bright-colored beads onto them, like this.

Tulips

To make tulips, cut out different shapes in step 1:

This shape makes a straight tulip.

To make a curved tulip, cut out this shape.

Glittery hearts giftwrap

Keep both pieces of paper.

1. To make a stencil, fold a piece of thick paper in half. Draw half a heart against the fold, then cut along the line.

This paper was brushed with glue, then gold glitter was sprinkled over it.

2. Mix some red paint with white glue on an old plate. Then, spread the paint on the plate a little with the back of a spoon.

Hold the stencil in place.

3. Lay the stencil on a large piece of thin paper. Dab the sponge into the paint, then over the heart, until it is filled with paint.

You can print hearts straight onto a gift box.

Sponge red and gold paint over the stencil, then sprinkle glitter all over the heart.

This heart was decorated with tiny beads.

You could fill a heart-shaped bag (see pages 18-19) with these love tokens as a Valentine gift.

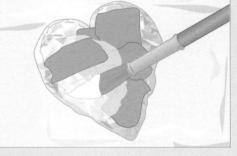

6. Press pieces of tissue paper onto the wet glue. Then, brush on more glue and press on more paper, until the heart is covered.

7. Leave the glue to dry completely. Then, mix some bright paint and white glue together well on an old plate.

Lay the heart on a newspaper.

8. Paint decorations on the heart with a thin paintbrush. Sprinkle glitter over the wet paint, shake off any excess and let it dry.

Valentine bracelet

1. Cut a long piece of ribbon that goes once around your wrist, with a little extra for tying on the bracelet.

Use different shades of paper if you have them.

2. Draw three hearts and two flowers on pieces of bright-colored paper. Cut them out, then bend the petals with your fingers, like this.

3. Using white glue, glue one heart onto the middle of the ribbon. Then, glue on the flowers and the other hearts, too.

4. Glue a sequin in the middle of each flower. Then, when the glue is dry, ask someone to tie the bracelet around your wrist.

Try gluing two flowers together, like this.

Use some of the ideas from this page on your bracelet.

Spiral heart twirlers

Start winding in the middle.

1. For the twirler, bend a pipe cleaner in half. Lay one half along a pencil, then tightly wind it around and around, like this.

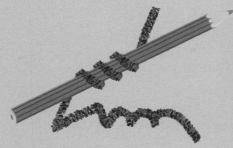

2. Slide the pipe cleaner off the pencil. Then, wind the other half of the pipe cleaner around and around the pencil, too.

Hold the layers of paper together as you cut.

3. Slide the pipe cleaner off the pencil. Then, fold a piece of paper in half and draw two hearts on it, like this. Cut out the hearts.

4. Spread glue on a heart. Lay one end of the twirler on it, then press another heart on top. Then, glue hearts onto the other end.

Use your twirler to decorate Valentine gifts.

5. For a bag, put a gift in the middle of a square of cellophane. Gather up the edges, like this, then twist a twirler around the bag.

Pretty heart bag

Use a piece of paper that is about the size of this page.

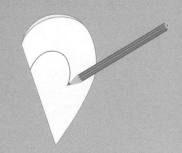

1. Fold a piece of paper in half and draw half a large heart against the fold. Then, holding the layers together, cut out the shape.

2. Unfold the heart and flatten it, then lay it on some thick paper. Draw around it twice. Then, cut out the hearts.

3. Fold the heart that you drew around in half again. Then, draw a second smaller half heart inside and cut along the line.

Lay the hearts on a newspaper.

The glue helps to keep the hearts together.

4. Open out the small heart that you have just cut out. Lay it on some paper. Draw around it twice, then cut out the hearts.

5. Brush white glue over the two smaller hearts. Sprinkle glitter over them, then glue on some sequins. Leave them to dry.

6. Glue the smaller hearts onto the big ones. Then, dab glue on the point of one of the big hearts and press the other one on top.

To add a spangly trim to your bag, glue sequins around the edge, like this.

7. Using one side of a hole puncher, make holes along both sides of the heart, but don't make holes all the way to the top.

You could glue
a plain heart
onto a striped
background.

To make a heart-
shaped card like
this one, glue a big
heart onto a card
and cut around it.

Sparkly heart love tokens

1. Cut a piece of kitchen foil that is about the size of this page. Then, scrunch it tightly in the middle, like this.

2. To make one side of the heart, gently scrunch one end of the foil in on itself. Then, bend it around, into the middle of the foil.

3. Scrunch the other end of the foil in the same way. Then, bend it around into the middle, to make a heart shape.

Lay the heart on some plastic foodwrap.

4. Press the heart with your hands, to squash the foil into a smooth shape. Make a point at the bottom of the heart.

5. Rip a piece of bright tissue paper into lots of small pieces. Then, brush part of the foil heart with white glue.

Try gluing on sequins or little paper shapes.

8. Cut a very long piece of thin ribbon. Then, starting at the middle of one side, thread the ribbon through the holes in the heart.

9. Cut two large circles from tissue paper. Fold them in half and push them into the bag. Then, tie the ribbon in a bow.

For a Valentine gift, fill a bag with chocolates or love tokens (see pages 14-15).

You could put a Valentine message in a heart bag.

Bright heart flowers

Make sure the straw isn't more than halfway up the heart.

1. Fold a piece of paper in half and draw half a heart against the fold. Then, keeping the paper folded, cut out the shape.

2. Open out the shape and lay it on some thick paper. Draw around it four times, then cut out the hearts you have drawn.

3. Tape a drinking straw near the bottom of one of the hearts, like this. Squash the end of the straw as you tape it.

This leaf was brushed with white glue and sprinkled with glitter.

The slots need to be the same length.

4. Glue another heart over the straw. Then, cut four thin strips of green paper. Tape them near the top of one of the other hearts.

5. Glue the final heart onto the heart with the strips, then cut a slot up into it. Then, cut a slot down into the heart with the straw.

You could give someone a bunch of heart flowers tied with a ribbon.

This gift tag was sprinkled with glitter when the paint was still wet.

Don't move the stencil.

4. Before the paint has dried, sprinkle red glitter over the left half of the heart. Gently press the glitter on with your fingers.

A mixture of painted hearts and glittery ones looks really pretty.

5. Move the stencil and print lots more hearts, all over the paper. Then, leave the paint to dry completely.

6. For a tag, lay the heart that you cut out in step 1 on some folded paper. Sponge paint over the tag, then sprinkle it with glitter.

Tissue paper flowers

Hold all the layers together as you cut.

1. To make the petals, fold a big piece of tissue paper in half. Fold the paper in half twice more, then draw a heart and cut it out.

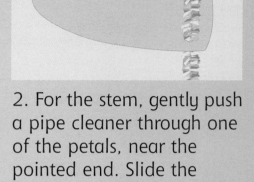

2. For the stem, gently push a pipe cleaner through one of the petals, near the pointed end. Slide the petal a little way down.

3. Thread the rest of the petals on in the same way. Then, gently spread the petals out around the stem, to make a flower.

4. Holding the petals from underneath, wrap a short piece of sticky tape around them and press it onto the stem, to secure the petals.

5. For a leaf, fold a piece of tissue paper in half. Draw a heart on it, then cut out the shape, keeping the paper folded.

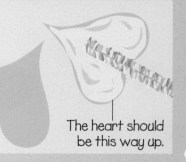

The heart should be this way up.

6. Cut another pipe cleaner in half. Spread glue on one of the leaves, then press the end of the pipe cleaner onto the glue.

To make a bouquet, tie lots of flowers together with a shiny ribbon.

You could use different shades of tissue paper for the flowers.

7. Press the other leaf over the top and leave the glue to dry. Then, gently brush white glue over the top of the leaf.

8. Sprinkle glitter over the wet glue and leave it to dry. Then, lay the leaf stem next to the main stem and twist them together tightly.

Lovebird decorations

Keep the paper folded as you cut.

To make a heart, glue a decorated foil heart onto a red one.

1. For the lovebird's body, fold a piece of thick paper in half. Draw a bird on it, then carefully cut out the shape.

2. Cut a rectangle of kitchen foil. Then, spread glue on the paper birds and press them onto the foil, facing each other.

The cuts in the border make the foil easier to bend.

Glue an eye and a beak onto each bird.

3. Cut around the birds, leaving a border. Make V-shaped cuts in the border and bend the foil over the edges of the birds.

4. Make paper eyes and beaks and glue them onto the birds. Then, using a blunt pencil, draw tiny hearts all over their bodies.

5. Tape a piece of ribbon onto the back of one of the birds, like this. Then, glue the other bird on top, lining up the edges.

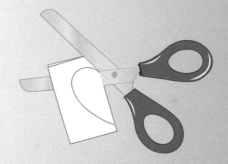

The double heart is for the wings.

6. For the wings and tail, fold a piece of thick paper in half. Draw half a heart against the fold, cut out the shape and open it out.

7. Lay the white heart on some thick red paper. Draw around it four times. Then, lay it next to one heart and draw around it again.

8. Cut out the shapes and erase the pencil lines. Then, cut up into the bottom of each of the single hearts and into the double heart.

You could make
a red bird with
a foil tail and
wings, too.

Make lots of
lovebirds and
hang them on
branches for
a Valentine
decoration.

9. Make three cuts at the
back of the bird and one in
the middle, like this. Then,
slide the tail feathers and
wings into the cuts.

Hearts and flowers cards

Give the card to someone when you see them, so that it doesn't get squashed in an envelope.

Make the other parts of the card while the glue

1. Brush a layer of white glue over a strip of paper. Then, sprinkle lots of glitter over the wet glue and leave it to dry.

To make this card, glue doves onto the glittery strips, then glue them onto a silver tree.

You could make a vase with flowers instead of hearts.

2. To make a vase for the front of the card, cut a vase shape and a heart from paper. Then, glue the heart onto the vase.

Use the ideas on these pages to make a gift tag.

3. Cut three small hearts from shiny paper and three bigger ones from pink paper. Then, glue the small hearts onto the bigger ones.

4. Cut the glittery paper into three thin strips. Then, with the glittery side facing up, glue the hearts onto the ends of the strips.

Make sure that the glittery strips are facing you.

5. Cut three long pieces of gift ribbon. Then, turn the vase over and tape the ribbons onto it. Tape on the glittery strips, too.

Put your thumb

6. To curl each piece of ribbon, hold it against some closed scissors, like this. Pull the ribbon firmly across the scissor blade.

7. Fold a piece of thick paper in half, to make a card. Glue the vase onto it. Then, bend the glittery strips with your fingers.

8. Draw lots of hearts on shiny paper. Cut them out and glue them around the vase. Glue on sequins.

Love bugs

1. For a bug's body, cut a piece of kitchen foil that is about the size of this page. Then, crush the foil to make a rounded body.

You need to make three pairs of legs.

2. For the legs, cut a third off three pipe cleaners. Bend the longer pieces into squashed 'M' shapes with feet sticking out, like these.

Cut off any foil that you don't need.

3. Tape the legs onto the body. Then, cut a strip of kitchen foil. Lay the foil over the legs and scrunch it tightly between them.

4. Rip lots of small pieces from pink tissue paper. Then, brush part of the love bug's body with white glue.

5. Press the pieces of tissue paper onto the wet glue. Then, brush on more glue and press on more paper, until the body is covered.

The wings should be about the same length as the body.

6. For the wings, fold a piece of thick paper in half. Draw a wing shape on it, then cut out the shape, through both layers.

Curve the
wings like this.

7. Curve the wings a little,
using your fingers. Then,
for the bug's feelers, cut
two thin, pointed strips
from thick paper.

You could cut out
heart-shaped
leaves for
your bug
to sit on.

Push in the
feelers when the
glue is still wet.

8. Glue the front ends of
the wings onto the body
and push the feelers under
them. Then, gently curl the
pointed ends of the feelers.

9. For eyes, cut circles from
paper, then glue smaller
circles in the middle. Glue
the eyes onto the bug and
decorate its wings.

10. Cut a small heart from
pink or red paper and write
a Valentine message on it.
Bend the card a little, then
slide it under the wings.

Try painting roses
in different sizes
and shades.

You could paint green
leaves in the spaces
between the roses.

Valentine roses giftwrap

The wax resists the paint.

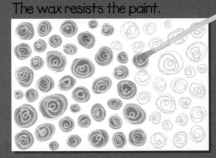

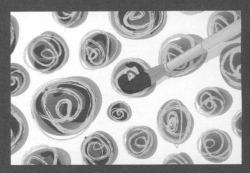

1. Using a wax crayon,
draw a rose on a big piece
of paper. Starting in the
middle, draw a spiral going
out and then back in again.

2. Draw lots more roses.
Then, using really watery
paint or ink, paint a round
blob over each rose. Leave
the paint to dry.

3. When the paint is dry,
paint over parts of the
roses with slightly darker
paint, like this. Then, leave
the paint to dry.

Photographic manipulation: Nick Wakeford • Images of flowers on pages 2-3 © Digital Vision • No part of this publication may be reproduced, stored in a retrieval system, or transmitted in any form or by any means, electronic, mechanical, photocopying, recording, or otherwise, without written permission of the publisher. For information regarding permission, write to Usborne Publishing Ltd., Usborne House, 83-85 Saffron Hill, London, EC1N 8RT, England. First published in Great Britain in 2005 by Usborne Publishing Ltd. • ISBN 0-439-78705-X • Copyright © 2005 by Usborne Publishing Ltd. All rights reserved. Published by Scholastic Inc., 557 Broadway, New York, NY 10012, by arrangement with Usborne Publishing Ltd. The name Usborne and the devices ⊕ ⊛ are trademarks of Usborne Publishing Ltd. SCHOLASTIC and associated logos are trademarks and/or registered trademarks of Scholastic Inc. • 12 11 10 9 8 7 6 5 4   6 7 8 9 10 11/0 • Printed in the U.S.A.   40 • First Scholastic printing, January 2006